W9-ABQ-861

THE Cool KING

PHOTOGRAPHY
BOB MORELAND

COMPILED BY
GER J. RIJFF

TEXT BY
JAN VAN GESTEL

atomium books

FOR
SCOTTY

COLOPHON

The editor and author are particularly
indebted to the following people and
institutions for their enthusiasm and support.

The St. Petersburg Times, Florida
The St. Petersburg Public Library, Florida
Photo restoration:
    New Move, Amsterdam

First published in the United States 1990 by

Atomium Books Inc.
Suite 300
1013 Centre Road
Wilmington, DE 19805.

First edition published in English, by Tutti
Frutti Productions, Amsterdam, Holland,1989
under the title "Elvis, The Cool King".

Printed in Belgium by Color Print Graphix.
First U.S. Edition
ISBN 1-56182-010-5
EAN 9 781561 820108
2 4 6 8 10 9 7 5 3 1

atomium books

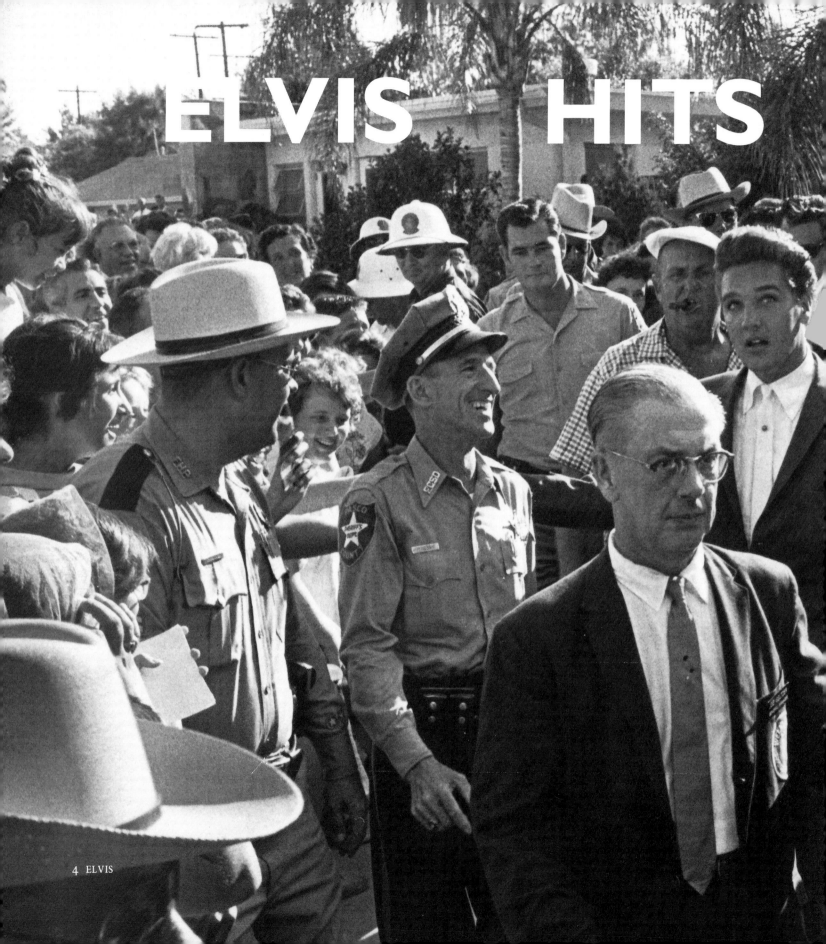

ELVIS   HITS

SUNCOAST

THE COOL KING 5

JUST BEFORE
ALL HELL
BREAKS LOOSE

There's a moment where time is suspended. Just after strapping on his guitar, and just before letting his slow gaze wander 'cross the audience, the girls in the front row sit transfixed. All of them have entered a no man's land of dreams unfulfilled, expectations that can't be put into words, and a yearning that races in time with the beat of their hearts. The one in the middle is supercharged like all the rest. Forgotten are the hours of waiting. The mad dash to get to the best seats. The barrage of hawkers selling tiny folders for fifty dollar cents. What a rook! Forgotten the disappointment on learning in the beginning of the show that Elvis wouldn't be coming on 'til last. Sure they'd yelled 'We want Elvis! We want Elvis!' but they knew it wouldn't do any good.

Now the man she wants stands in front of her. Suddenly the oppressive August heat seems to lift in the Florida Theater in downtown St. Petersburg. To outsiders that one immeasurable moment might come across like the calm before the storm. But that's not where she is. She's right in the eye of the storm, right there with him. Where nothing else matters. Glued to her chair, mouth hanging open, trying hard to believe her eyes.

The sparkling of a diamond ring accompanies the slow ascent of his hand up the microphone stand. And as the hand firmly cups the ribbed brushed chromium microphone her knuckles turn white from clutching her bag tighter. Almost imperceptibly he lifts his gaze and she drinks in the cool blue flash of his eyes. Her body is taut and she's got goose bumps all over.

'Well since mah baby left me...' She's swept up in the hurricane. She feels but can't hear herself screaming in a high-pitched wail that's pure joy and pain. Sounds of an electric guitar thunder low and pining like nothing she's ever heard before. He snaps his leg and she can feel tears coming. Her heart's pounding madly as if to push the plodding beat of the song to a frenzy. There's no one she can turn to for help but him. The girl next to her yells in her ear 'Oh, isn't he dreamy!' But she doesn't notice. A king supremely cool has stepped into the no man's land and conquered it in an instant. And his rule sweeps all before it. And her soul swoons.

When interviewed some thirty years after they'd attended one or more of the twenty four shows Elvis gave in Florida from August 3 to August 11, 1956, most of the women's memories of the event are fragmentary at best. The one thing they all seem to agree on is the screaming. Beyond that, recollections are mostly vague. Only occasionally are they specific, as in the case of two teenage girlfriends who loved Elvis' records, but were shocked when they saw how he spat on stage. They thought he was being incredibly rude. Reliability is the issue here. Others who were involved directly in the Presley phenomenon are not that much more reliable either. Elvis' original producer, Sam Phillips, seems to have developed over the years a neatly structured tale of how it all went. It's a tale that in its comprehensiveness contrasts oddly with a recollection of D.J. Fontana, Elvis' drummer in the early years. When he was interviewed in the early seventies he once mentioned 'Kissin' Cousins' as one of the first few movies Elvis made.

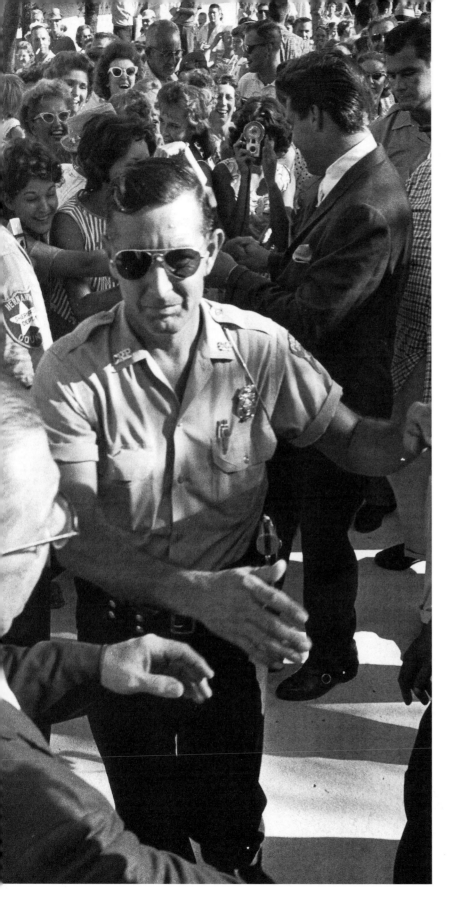

Of course, time takes its toll on all our memories, and what's pressed between the pages of our minds is a highly personal (and limited) selection indeed. And if we acknowledge the continuing existence of a Great Divide between those who love Elvis and those who don't, and we look to the other side for more objective views, we don't fare much better. Perhaps the opposition between fans and non-fans was more clearly drawn in the Fifties, and journalists in particular felt called upon to write from a completely condescending if not outright dismissive point of view. However, there was one kind of journalist who couldn't help conveying the truth. These were, of course, the photographers. With their cameras they captured Elvis countless times as he faced another crowd. Bob Moreland was one of them.

Moreland shot the photographs on the preceding and following pages on July 30, 1961, and they are the only reliable witnesses we'll probably ever have of that Sunday. Bob Moreland had aimed his camera at Elvis earlier. But that had been five years before (*photographs from page 31 onward*), and he must have wondered about the change in appearance of the erstwhile rocker. And some setting to see him back in!

Because here we are in Weeki Wachee Springs (No, not whacky but whetchee) and boy do
we have sunshine. The 'we' in this case are the citizens of Weeki Wachee, and they've
invited Elvis to honor him for his achievements. It's a well publicized event, so when Elvis
arrives around 4:00 p.m. (page 7) there's over 15,000 fans at hand to give him a rousing and
crushing welcome. Naturally, and as usual, Elvis' manager, Colonel Tom Parker, is close at
hand too, sweating like a pig, lightning-rod Havana stuck firmly in his mouth. There's no
doubt who's running the show and it sure ain't no Weeki Wachean.

Where in 1956 gaining publicity at all costs was the objective, whether it be through
notoriety alone, now in 1961 Parker has finely honed the art of the media game.
So when he brings out Elvis it's certainly not for live shows anymore.
Parker wants to let the people know that they're not just dealing with a recording star,
but with a big time movie star as well.

The whole publicity exercise has been meticulously planned in advance. Two hours have been set aside for an event that could have been taken straight from some scenario for an electioneering campaign American style. There's a big crowd present, plenty of kids to buss, dignitaries to meet, and some surprises that will go down well with the press. Thanks to Bob Moreland's second assignment to cover Presley for the St. Petersburg Times, the photographs collected for this book present us with a fascinating study in contrasts. Kids eagerly waiting for a quick peck on the cheek clutch photographs with an Elvis image of the Fifties. One can't help but wonder if the Colonel has been getting rid of old stock here.

There's a contrast too in the coolness displayed by Elvis as he undergoes rather than participates in the event. Although here he's accompanied by actress Anne Helm on his left, and his father with his second wife on the right, it seems unlikely Elvis would ever have chosen to visit Weeki Wachee Springs had it been up to him. Because this place is geared more to families for a day out than it is to a guy who when he started out as a tough rock 'n' roll singer had very proper Florida girls rip the shirt off his back. But that was a long time ago and now he once more obliges and takes a seat for something that management is sure he'll really enjoy. This place not only boasts magnificent boat rides, you see, but also offers real live Mermaids.

Nothing more is expected of Elvis than that he be present, smile, sign autographs and generally make a good impression. His publicity profile has changed immensely in the mere five years since he burst on the national scene and left middle class America reeling in his wake. But now nineteen hundred fifty six is merely a memory, a memory superseded on the personal plane by the loss of his mother in 1958 and two interminable years spent in the Army. We see a mature man now, but one who to our irreparable loss is not allowed to express his growth through the art form for which he's become famous. Instead he is constricted to the numbing medium of matinee movies. And on his one day off from shooting one of those movies, 'Follow That Dream,' he's engaged on a visit to an attraction that would turn on anyone's waterworks.

The boatride that's been scheduled is just an introduction to one of Barker Parker's special effects. He's approved a show in a large underwater tank and it features the first and only appearance of the Elvis Presley underwater fan club. Anyone may be forgiven for never having heard of this fan club before. It's a perfect example of what could be called Colonel Parker's Genuine Imitation of the Real Thing. From his point of view artistic credibility is intellectual drivel. The focus is on money exclusively. Hence the change in career after Elvis' demob, a change that was already contractually agreed upon whilst Elvis was still in Germany.
Of course, good money could be made with live performances, but not nearly as fast as by making a string of B movies. Add revenues from soundtrack recordings, movies and albums boosting each other, and you just can't lose.

The period of 1960 to 1968 in Elvis' career has often been sneered at by critics and fans alike, each contending that Elvis should've stood up and demanded better material to work with, viz., better movie plots and a good repertoire of songs. This is ignoring one basic aspect, the commercial one. When Elvis concurred it was not like the sort of dummy he portrayed in the movie 'Follow That Dream.' (How does one dream up a name like Toby Kwimper?) In 1963 he remarked on the subject of the matinee stuff: 'I've done eleven movies so far and they've all made money. A certain type of audience likes me. I entertain them with what I'm doing. I'd be a fool to tamper with that kind of success.' It's not difficult to perceive behind this kind of statement the truck driver that miraculously struck gold. Both Elvis and the Colonel always played it by ear. Right from the beginning there persisted a basic doubt as to how long the whole thing would last. There never was such a thing as career planning. So is it a coincidence that here we see Elvis surrounded by Weeki Wachee mermaids, while he is signing his latest release at the time, the album 'Something For Everybody'

In the VIP room the usual line up of local big wigs, representatives of the press and an array of gushing females files past Elvis. A special whisper is reserved for photographer Bob Moreland's twelve year old daughter, Michele. Then the star will once more be whisked off by dark-suited members of the Memphis Mafia, to return to the town of Clear River, on the Gulf of Mexico. Shooting for 'Follow That Dream' will resume on Monday. On that same day Moreland in his dark room will discover that some of the portraits he shot of a withdrawn Elvis 'turned out real nice' (*overleaf*).

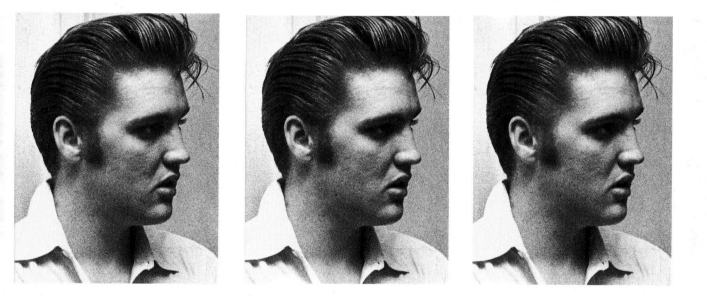

It's Sunday the fifth of August 1956 in Tampa, Florida. Elvis has arrived there from Miami, where he's given six shows in the two preceding days. Billboard magazine dated August 4, 1956, notes the entry on its 'Top 100' chart of the record 'Hound Dog' at number 24 for the week ending July 25th. The single will stay in the charts for seven months. It's the second pot of gold he's found in half a year. And now they've come to see for themselves. The Seratoma Civic Club has sponsored two shows at the Fort Homer Hesterly Armory in Tampa. Tickets are priced one dollar fifty for general admission and two dollars for reserved seats. The setting is typical of the sort of halls Elvis now plays. It's primitive. The stage is composed of huge boxes, the number of which can be varied to accommodate different needs. These boxes tend to be wobbly. The sound system is composed of two microphones and two amplifiers, fifty watts each.

'Well, it's what I feel, I guess.
Some of it's real; some of it's made up.'

There is no sophisticated light show. There's no dimming of house lights or a strong spot light piercing the dark to pick out the star on stage. The line up of the show forms a truly unreal backdrop to what is to be the high point. It's the kind of variety getup that is just about acceptable for some sort of Southern hoedown. With Frankie Connors, a local celebrity from Tampa, acting as emcee and singing Irish ballads you would never want to take the package up North in the first place. Then there's The Jordanaires and magician Phil Maraquin. The whole thing is corny and takes a godawful long time. In no way does it prepare for what follows, in fact, it's hard to think of a shriller contrast. After sitting through about one and a half hours of outdated entertainment the audience is confronted with a wholly new form that rises like a phoenix from the ashes of the old one. Kids call it Cool.

Under their very eyes a revolution rages. Amplifiers are strained to the limit and brawl distortion. Unmoved by bedlam the lead guitar player stands, minding his pickin'. Sweat pours down the face of the stocky guy playing double bass and the fool. He hollers. The singer moans low. A set of drums is being stroked, then punished. The whole thing's an outrage. Look man, the singer seems to be implying, show me any limit and we'll break right through it. Let's all get gone. Why, don't it feel good?

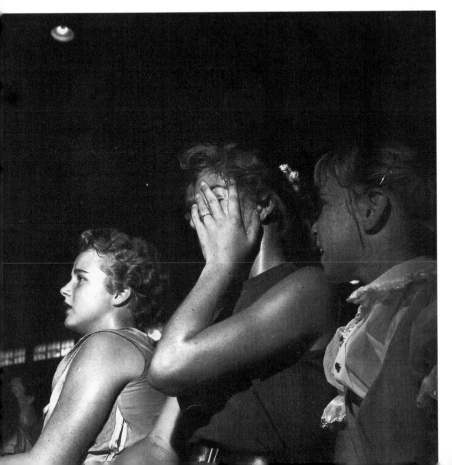

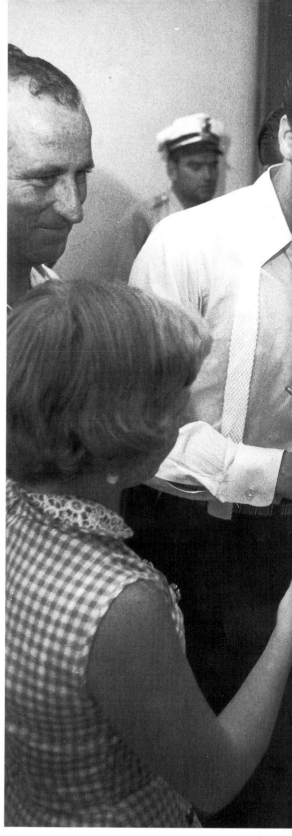

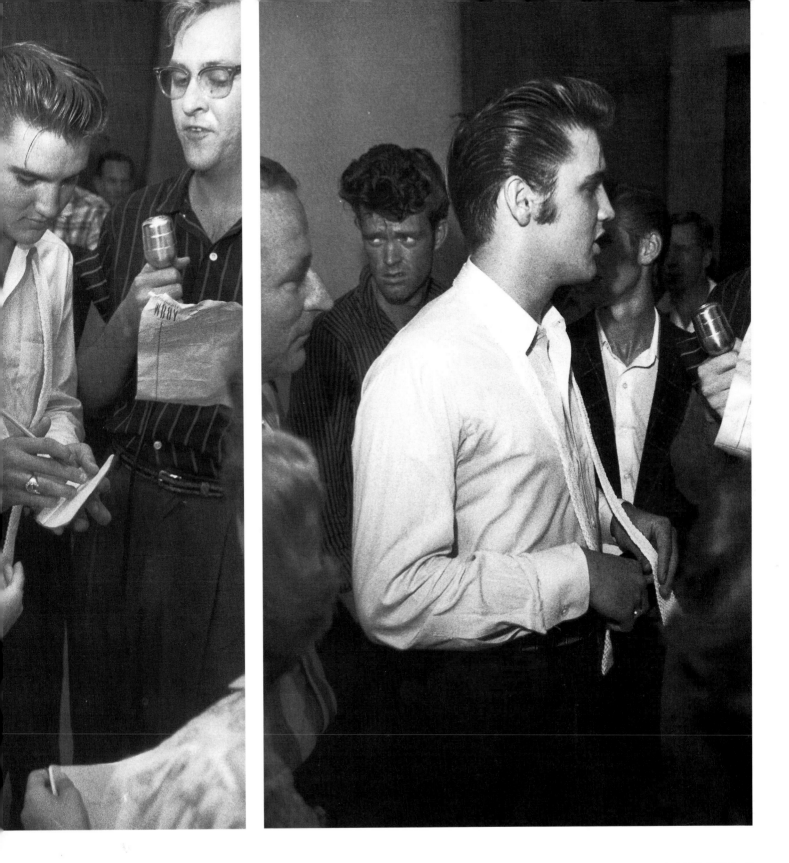

At this stage the world of rock 'n' roll is self-contained and exclusive. This poses some sort of problem for those outside it. Authorities, teachers, clergymen and parents are baffled. Why should you call a long haired, pimplefaced young hood out of Memphis a cool cat? But they're not baffled for long. So the sheriff of Tampa wanders into the dressing room to shake hands with the guy. The president of the Seratoma Civic Club is more than pleased with the takings at the gate. And from the press corps there's Ann Rowe from the St. Petersburg Times. She wants an interview with what she will call 'the biggest thing in show business today.'

Anne Rowe's findings appear in the August 6 issue of the St. Petersburg Times under the heading: BROOM-SWEEPING ELVIS A REGULAR GUY. The broom-sweeping occurs as she enters the dressing room some time before Elvis is to go on for his first Tampa show. Apart from the customary description of what Elvis wears ('dressed as sharp as a cat in black pegged pants, striped belt, blue shirt, white tie, maroon jacket and white buck shoes') Ann Rowe's article unlike most of the others written on the subject around that time, lacks all negativity. She doesn't put down his Southern accent. She doesn't once use the word 'antics' for Elvis' movements during the show, nor has the word 'suggestive' crept into her vocabulary.

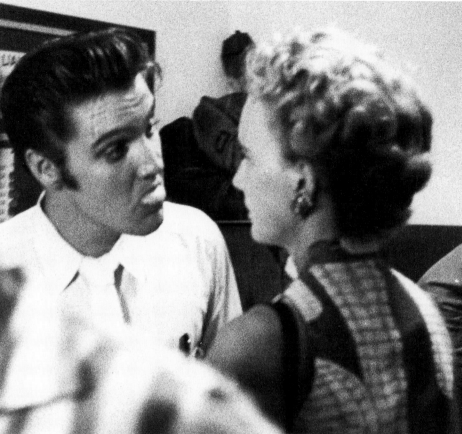

Ann Rowe spends about an hour with Elvis. It's a good thing
somebody has warned her 'to proceed with caution' in his
presence. Elvis obviously likes her and gives her the full
treatment. Of course Miss Rowe won't write about that part.
She will write that initially he appears nervous before the show.
But soon the tables will turn. Elvis turns on his will 'o the wisp
charm. One minute he's looking deep in Ann's eyes, the next
he's talking to somebody else. He's just goofing around.

The next thing Ann Rowe knows Elvis is trying to pull her close to him. He moves
faster than lightning. Before she knows it he's kissing her and she has a hard time
staying objective. What's real and what's made up? She's meeting the public Elvis. Like
on stage he moves through a whole gamut of emotions in quicksilver succession, in
physical proximity to a woman like Ann Rowe he's not to be pinned down either.
Courteous and polite don't apply here. One minute he's out on the make, the next
he's stepping outside and starts playing with some toddlers.

On the basis of photographs like these and those on the following pages Elvis has often been criticized for over conforming and trying to please all people. Ann Rowe notes, however, that he really seems to enjoy playing with these kids, putting them at ease. Only moments later he'll give an interview to a local Tampa radio station, WALT, then talk to some fans and curious onlookers and fool around with this journalist woman some more. Here we're coming close to one of the main nodes that make up the enigma called Elvis. Having a good time is used as defense mechanism against too many people laying a claim on him.

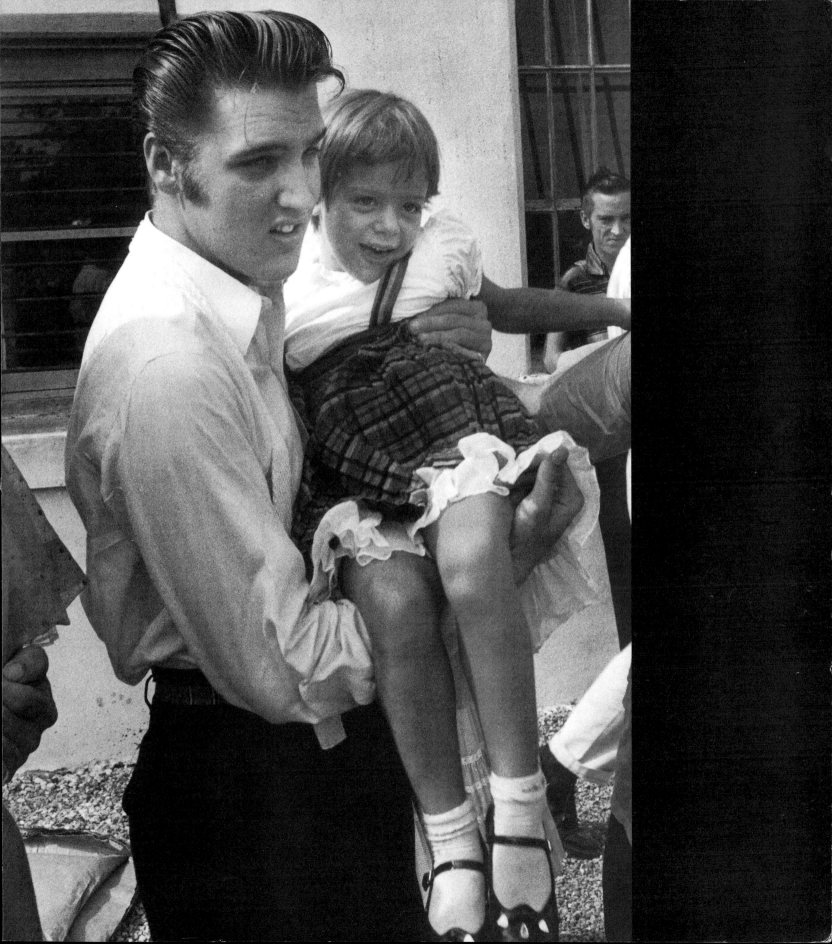

So why not take a quick lunch consisting of a bowl of ice cream and coffee from a paper cup, whilst being interviewed? By now he knows most of the questions by heart anyway and the ones he doesn't know he'll deal with as they come along. And although the moment he'll have to go on is now approaching fast, Elvis stays cool as ever. Here he's riding an unprecedented wave of success and all the time maintaining a stance of total relaxation. It's the contradiction between this poise implying total control and the other half of his public persona which on stage carries on crazy as a coon and in complete self abandon that baffles all outsiders. Just how much of it is real and how much is made up?

The fundamental dichotomy of a by all accounts basically shy young man hitting the big time almost overnight is one that is lost on the representatives of the American press at that time. The preoccupation with results rather than with the processes which led to them prevents them from really entering into the secret bond between Elvis and his fans. The main point for the journalists is to pigeonhole this youngster in some way that will take the sting out of his being there. Hence Ann Rowe reassures her readers that Elvis is just a regular guy. Nothing could be farther from the truth. No regular guy in the fifties would dare act on stage like he does. No regular guy would be driven to search for that unique sense of freedom which in his singing reaches out to all who want to hear.

They want to catch every word he says. They surge around him in the merciless heat, shoving and pushing 'til tempers are strained and hard words are flashed. Is he bemused by their insistence or apprehensive about these adults behaving like kids? If he's guarded he don't show it. If they're silly, why, let them be. There's no one comes close.

He's from another world where a man may be moved to sing like a fire in the sun. Moved to burn the nights on desolate highways. Moved to be born again everytime he steps out on stage. So if they want to find out what he's really like they might as well ask his constant companions Junior or cousin Billy. What could be learned from a shrug of their shoulders?

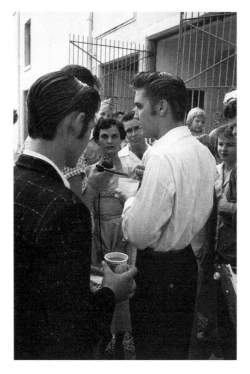

It's not from her interview that the diligent truth-seeker Miss Ann gets to the heart of the matter. Sure he gives her answers and then some, but the full truth will only be revealed inside the theater. It prompts Ann Rowe to write that evening: 'Elvis displayed his terrific showmanship. It was more than obvious that he loved every scream and yell and…every minute on that stage. He wrestled with the mike, breaking two apart in his frenzy, and finally, with perspiration pouring down his face, he practically tore his jacket off and let go on two more numbers.'

If there's one aspect of Elvis' style that immediately appealed to the American press, it must be his love of cars. So they describe him as 'four caddie Elvis.' To them it may be a gimmick, to Elvis it's as real as a ride on the fairground dodgems. In America in the Fifties a shining set of wheels is a status symbol of awesome power to the young. Once he's got the money for it Elvis

becomes car consumer first class. This ten thousand dollar baby is the latest addition. He bought this white Lincoln Continental two days before, in Miami. Jokingly he confides to Ann Rowe he bought it 'because I couldn't very well appear on Ed Sullivan's show if I wasn't driving his sponsor's product, could I?' (Elvis was booked for his first appearance on the Ed Sullivan television show only four weeks later, on September 9th.)

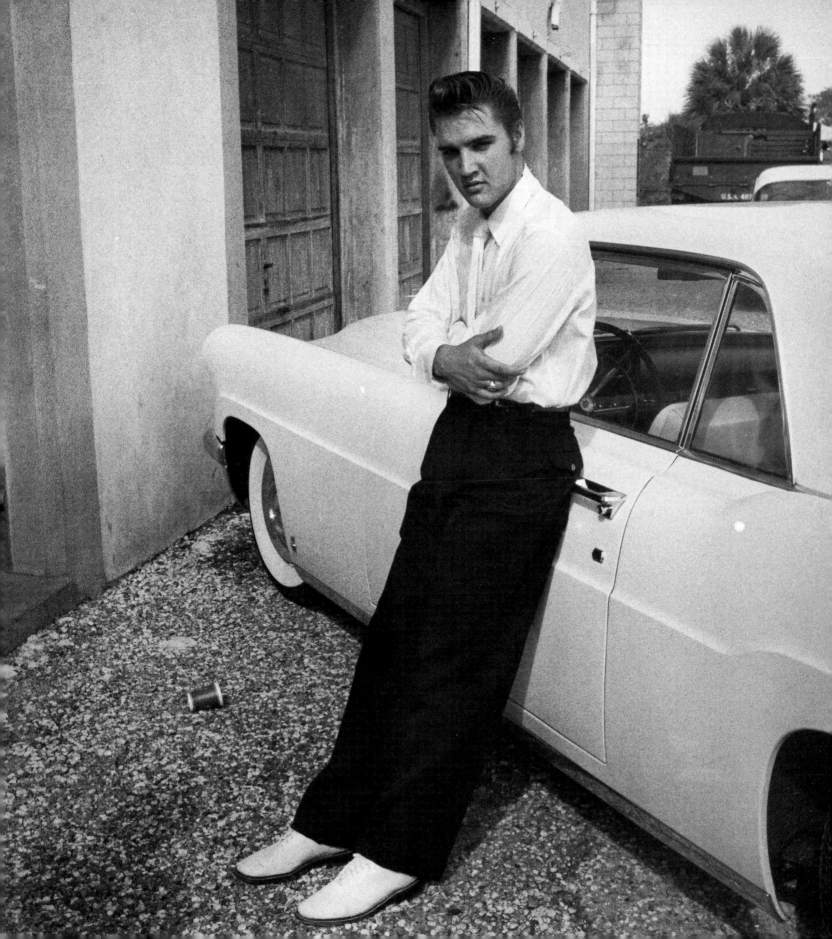

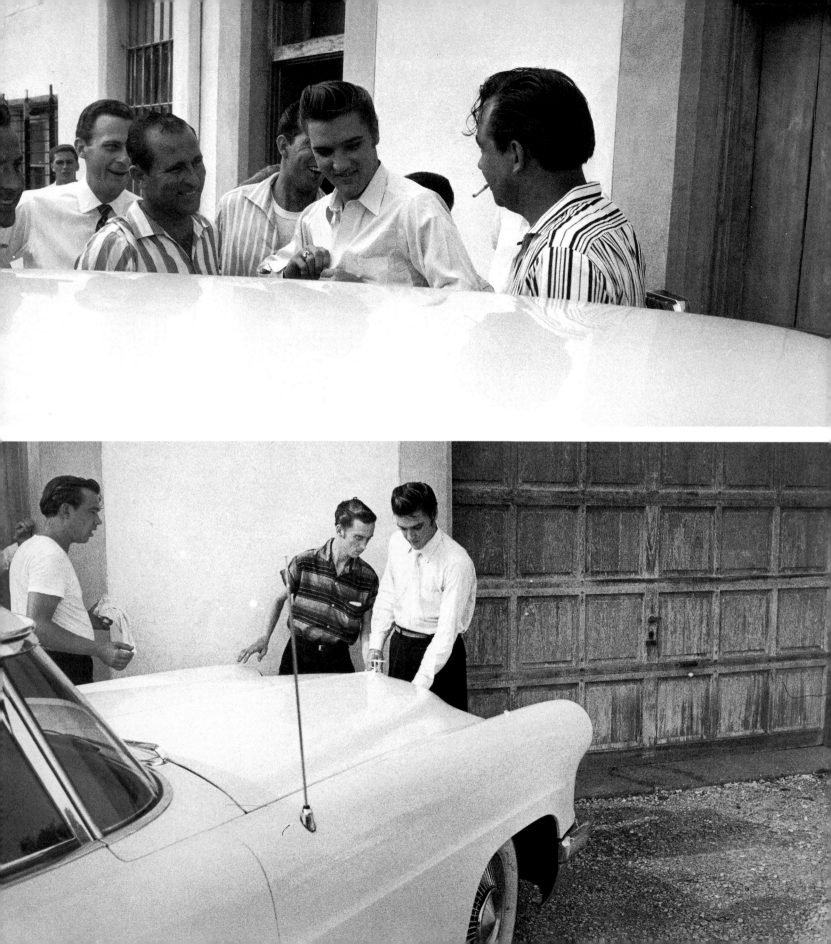

More than ten thousand people attend the two shows Elvis gives in Tampa. The Lincoln Continental
will take Elvis and a couple of cronies to Lakeland, where he's booked for three shows at the
Polk Theater for Monday, August 6th. That same Monday Ed Sullivan is involved in a car crash,
sustaining injuries that will prevent him from hosting Elvis's appearance on his show.
Not all sets of wheels are shining in the States that day.
But there's no stopping Elvis. Monday night he leaves Lakeland after three more sellout
performances, with a total attendance of 5,500. And heads down another highway,
destination St. Petersburg.

"Just rocking and reeling,
we'll get that feeling...
down in the alley."

Journalists have renamed it St. Presleyburg for the occasion. A delapidated back alley serves as the artist's entrance. Round the corner is the main entrance to the Florida Theater, where hundreds of fans have already lined up for hours. It's one o'clock and the first show won't start 'til three thirty p.m.

Under the more or less vigilant eye of some of the forty-five regular cops at hand, fans are admitted to the theater in small groups. Lightly skipping or in full trot, all betray pure excitement. And then, one and a half hours later, the supreme moment arrives. Sing to us. Take us along to another world full of music that's straight, open, and free. How the head spins as this music begins. Even if they've listened to the recorded version of the show's opener, Heartbreak Hotel, a hundred times before, it won't have prepared them for what's unleashed on them now.

This is the raw Elvis. He won't be on stage for much more than twenty minutes. He'll do seven songs. But those are plain statistics that don't have any bearing on what happens in that time. The performance is an all out assault on all the preconceptions that make up America's middle class morality. Only the day before the St. Petersburg Times carries a small article on how five carloads of 'Negroes' had dared to sunbathe on neighboring Sarasota's all-white Lido beach. And here's this guy not just carrying on like one, but actually sounding like one. And that ain't all. He spits and belches. You can't make head or tail of what he says between songs. And then he shimmies around with the mike as if he's got something going with it. If you hadn't seen it with your own eyes you'd never believe anything so vulgar could be possible. Thus the non-plussed outsiders.

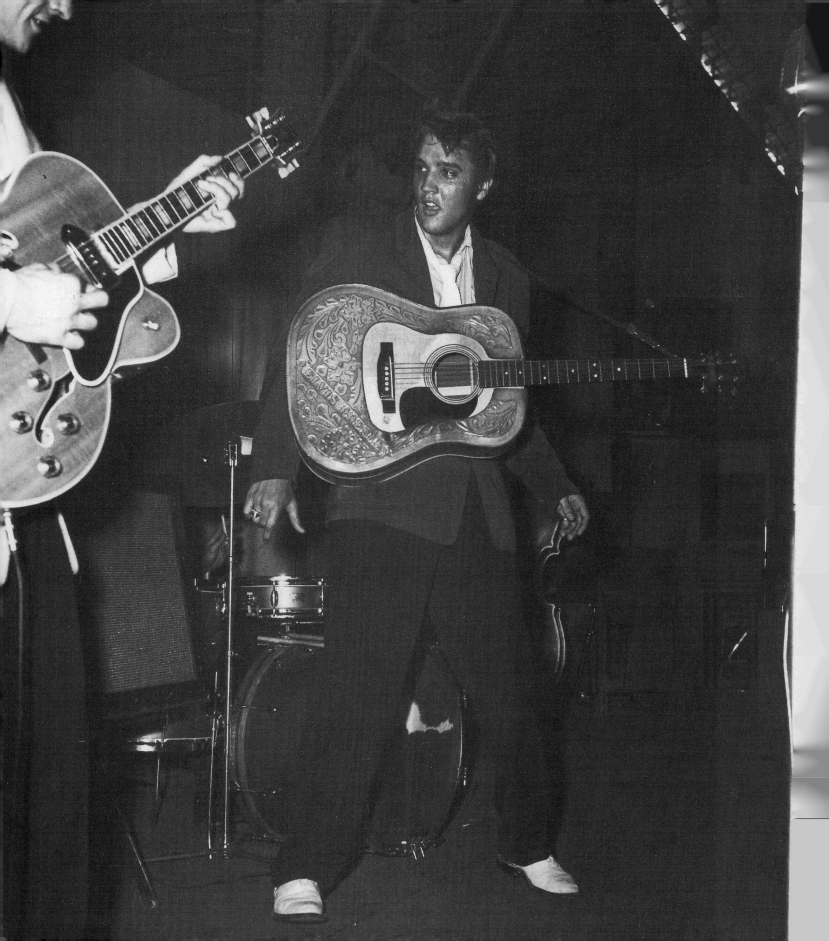

To most of the 2,000 odd
spectators Elvis represents
the embodiment of all that's
lacking in their lives. Here's
a real sense of adventure,
and a complete break with
conventions. And it's all
carried across in a
swashbuckling style which
as the American rock critic
Greil Marcus noted partakes
as much from Erroll Flynn as
it does from blues singers.
But all attempts at
categorization are futile.
He's neither strictly
country, nor strictly blues.
He can belt out a rocker
one minute, and croon and
swoon through a ballad the
next. The only constants in
the performance ('sure
hope you like the show so
far') are a sense of fun and
mischievousness. In his mad
dash for freedom nothing is
to be taken seriously for
too long, himself included.

During every live performance in 1956 there's a delectable moment of pure detachment where Elvis summarily disposes of his guitar. It's a cool gesture implying another break with all forms of constraint. Here's this instrument which has gotten a rough treatment so far at best. Now it's a hindrance to a further physical exploration of what they've all come here for. There's a neat symmetrical counterpart to this gesture just before the closing song, Hound Dog. Then Elvis will get rid of his green jacket, as if that too is only holding him back from the business at hand.

But they'll have to wait for that one.

Some thirty years on the structure of a typical Elvis concert in the Fifties can be analysed easily. The long wait through the rest of the package, with mediocrity as its keynote, brings the crowd's expectations to fever pitch. Then it's time for the star. Elvis and band deliver seven songs, each of which has been the subject of meticulous rehearsals before finally being recorded. During numerous live performances the songs have furthermore been sharpened for maximum impact. There's Bill Black's clowning. There's the unexpected and almost anarchic drum-rolls by D.J. Fontana. Scotty's precision picking that keeps things from falling apart at the seams. The whole thing's a well oiled machine, a fully professional outfit. And yet these considerations offer nothing by way of explaining the resulting ecstasy, the sheer magic by which this young man from Memphis skyrockets from regional to national and then worldwide fame. To this day the mystery endures.

The exhaustion after each show is not made up. Yet there's not a moment's
respite. Another interviewer is waiting anxiously while Elvis restores
his quiff to full regal splendor.

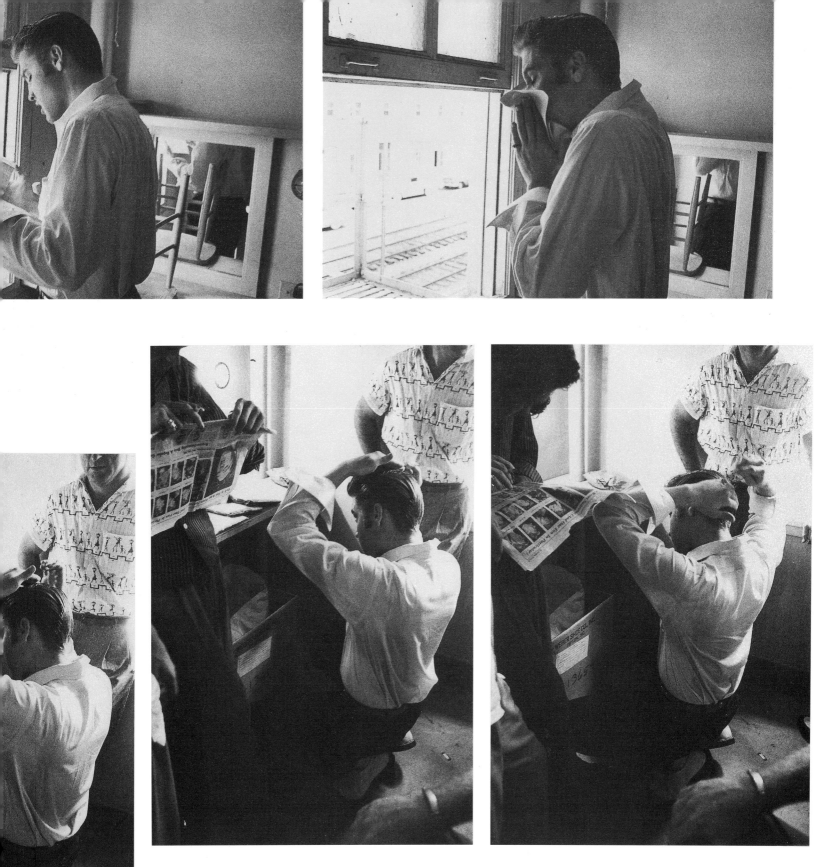

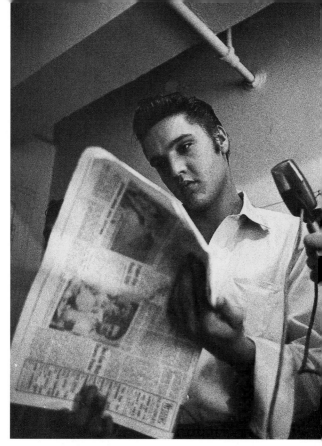

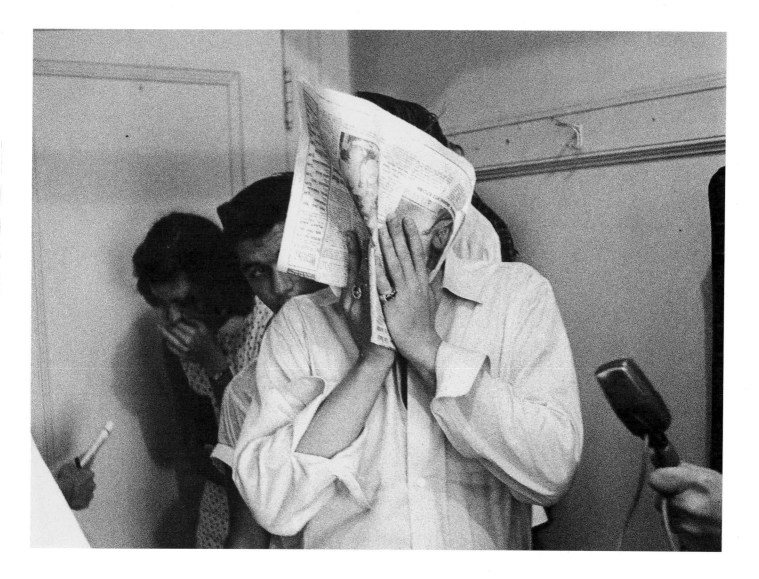

Someone's brought in a copy of
that day's St. Petersburg Times
with the Ann Rowe article on Elvis
in Tampa, accompanied by Bob
Moreland's photographs. If anyone
expected that a nearly full page
article is not to be sneezed at,
they're in for a real surprise!

In the meantime life goes on outside the theater. There's plenty of people waiting for a glimpse of this singer they're all talking about, and in the resulting crush a young girl faints. An ambulance shows up in a matter of minutes, by which time rumors of the incident will further have fuelled the imagination of those of the press who'd rather have this whole darn rock 'n' roll thing over by tomorrow. Certainly, in their case, tomorrow would prove to be a long time indeed.

Sure thing, they'll need all the COOL air-conditioning they can get when this king comes to town. If FLASH is the question, this guy is the answer. So go, man, go, in the face of wide-eyed wonder. Speak to the guys and tell 'em you showed her how. Sway to the beat when the screaming gets high. Hold to the here, the electrical heartbeat. And rock 'til they're gone, and can take it no more.

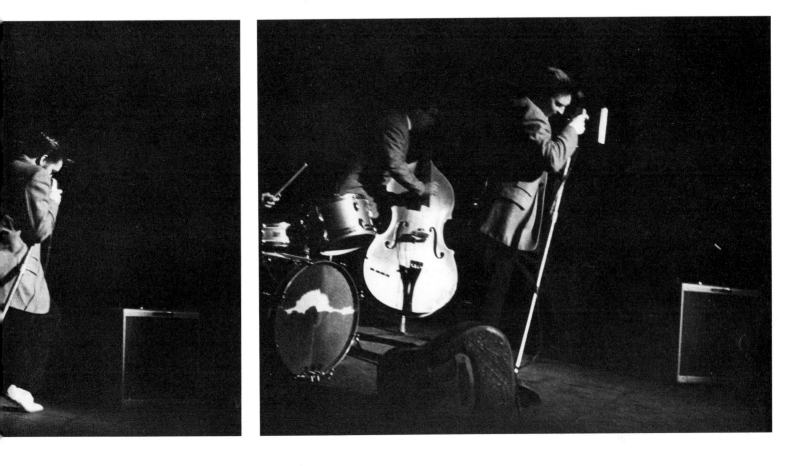

Each of the live performances by Elvis in the Fifties represents a step in the emergence
of a completely new art form. An art form that will ultimately penetrate to all corners
of the globe. Elvis sets its standards singlehandedly. Nowadays, going on to the Nineties,
it would take a whole army of bands to approximate the range of emotional effects that
Elvis effortlessly crams into a twenty minutes' show. Somehow that richness of feeling,
drawn from hidden wellsprings, transcends the confines of the old Florida Theater
and comforts us still.